Father, Bless Me Indeed

A Devotional Reading of Bible Blessings

Gladys Ogoti

TEACH Services, Inc.
PUBLISHING
www.TEACHServices.com • (800) 367-1844

World rights reserved. This book or any portion thereof may not be copied or reproduced in any form or manner whatever, except as provided by law, without the written permission of the publisher, except by a reviewer who may quote brief passages in a review.

The author assumes full responsibility for the accuracy of all facts and quotations as cited in this book. The opinions expressed in this book are the author's personal views and interpretations, and do not necessarily reflect those of the publisher.

This book is provided with the understanding that the publisher is not engaged in giving spiritual, legal, medical, or other professional advice. If authoritative advice is needed, the reader should seek the counsel of a competent professional.

Copyright © 2019 Gladys Ogoti
Copyright © 2019 TEACH Services, Inc.
ISBN-13: 978-1-4796-0991-8 (Paperback)
ISBN-13: 978-1-4796-0992-5 (ePub)
Library of Congress Control Number: 2018967695

Unless otherwise indicated, all Scripture quotations are from the New King James Version® (NKJV), copyright © 1982 by Thomas Nelson. Used by permission. All rights reserved.

The Holy Bible New International Version®. (NIV). Copyright © 1973, 1978, 1984 by International Bible Society. All rights reserved.

Published by

INTRODUCTION

Oh, that You would bless me indeed, and enlarge my territory, that Your hand would be with me, and that You would keep me from evil, that I may not cause pain!

The Bible tells about Jabez praying for a blessing. The circumstances surrounding his life demanded that he seek a blessing from God. After determining that I wanted to pray for a blessing from God, I paused and asked myself: What do I really want from God? Which blessing do I seek from Him?

Many times, I realize that whenever I pray for a blessing, I am asking for something I can hold in my hands, something physical. But then I read again Jabez's prayer and noted that he asked for a physical blessing in the second part of his prayer. This inspired me to go into the Scriptures to find out what the Bible says about being blessed, what the conditions are for being blessed, and what are the outcomes of being blessed. I looked up the verses that emphasize being blessed. The little book You hold in Your hands is the result of my searching and supplicating the Lord to *"bless me indeed."*

"And God blessed them, saying, 'Be fruitful and multiply.'"
Genesis 1:22

This is the first time the word "blessed" is used in the Bible. Here God is blessing the first couple on earth with the ability to have children.

Holy Father, I do realize that I am already blessed. So, as I pray for blessings, I want to thank You for the blessings I already have in You.

Thank You for the children You have given me. Multiply in me the spiritual gifts that You have given me and help me to be fruitful in helping others to know that they are blessed. Bring to fulfillment Your promise to Your people who seek children.

> *"I will bless those who bless you, and I will curse him who curses you; and in you all the families of the earth shall be blessed."*
> *Genesis 12:3*

This was a blessing to Abraham when he was called to leave his home. God gave him the assurance of protection.

What a blessing to know again that I am blessed in Abraham, that You promised to bless even my family through him! Lord, I am grateful for Your grace, which is all-inclusive. Cause me to have the faith of Abraham. Grant that I may be a blessing to future generations. Let all who come behind me find me faithful. Bless me with unwavering faith, and make me a servant humble and meek.

> Grant that I may be a blessing to future generations.

"Now it shall come to pass, if you diligently obey the voice of the LORD your God, to observe carefully all His commandments which I command you today, that the LORD your God will set you high above the nations of the earth. And all these blessings shall come upon you and overtake you, because you have obeyed the voice of the LORD your God."
Deuteronomy 28:1, 2

Is it possible that I am standing in the way of Your blessings? My Lord, please show me my shortcomings, and let Your kindness lead me to repentance. Help me know Your voice and hearken to it when I hear it.

Teach me to understand Your commandments. Forgive me where I have transgressed Your law. Lead me in the paths of righteousness. Help me to seek to do Your will. Work in me to help me realize this in my life.

> *"Blessed shall you be in the city,
> and blessed shall you be in the country."*
> **Deuteronomy 28:3**

I am amazed by Your love. When I lived in the country, I thought that Your blessing was upon those who lived in the city. I looked at the physical privileges they had, like water, electricity, and good roads. Now I live in the city, and I feel that those who live in the country are blessed. They are not prone to the temptations of civilization in the city. Now, Lord, as I read Your Word, I thank You for the assurance, that, if I keep Your commandment, I shall be blessed in the city and in the country. I believe Your Word; I am blessed wherever I am because You are with me.

> *"Blessed shall be the fruit of your body."*
> *Deuteronomy 28:4*

I rejoice in Your promise to bless the fruit of my body—the fruit of my womb. Now I present to You each of the children that You have placed in my care. They are Your children; I am only an instrument that You are using to raise them up. Bless them with an understanding of Your law. Cause them to walk in Your statutes. Fill them with the Holy Spirit and revive them in Your word.

Bless them in their academic endeavors. Make them a positive influence on the people that You bring into their lives. Let their lives be a blessing to us as their parents and to the community they live in. Bless them with the gift of discernment and with wisdom to enable them to make good moral choices. Live out Your life within them and have Your way in their lives.

"Blessed shall be ... the produce of your ground and the increase of your herds, the increase of your cattle, and the offspring of your flocks."
Deuteronomy 28:4

Whereas I realize that I do not have livestock, I thank You for the treasure that You have given. I commit my work into Your hands. Increase my nursing skills—the vocation that You have given me—and give me understanding as I minister to the sick who are placed under my care. Make me a blessing to my co-workers and an instrument of Your peace. Let no one be lost because of negligence on my part. Grant that many will see You in my service and give glory to Your name.

*"Blessed shall be your basket
and your kneading bowl."
Deuteronomy 28:5*

    I have seen this blessing in my life. Right now, I can only praise You for Your bountiful blessings. However, I wish to offer my supplication to You. Keep me faithful in returning to You what You place in my basket. Help me to not be selfish but to share that which You have entrusted into my stewardship. Even so Father, we still have needs as a family. We pray that You meet them according to Your will. Close all unnecessary avenues that will make us use up the resources You give us. Give us contentment and bless us with generous hearts.

*"Blessed shall be you when you come in,
and blessed shall you be when you go out."
Deuteronomy 28:6*

    I will be confident wherever I go because I know that I have Your promise. Help me to not be afraid to go on Your errands, be they at home or away from home. In the words of the famous hymn, I can safely go anywhere with You, Lord. I shall fear no danger "for thou art with me."

    I am so thankful that You have promised to walk with me until the end of the age. Cause me to have a spirit of gratitude and to have my house full of praise. Your hand has led, and it is leading and will lead me on. Even though friends may fail, You are my anchor. Anywhere with my Lord is homey.

"The LORD will command the blessing on you in your storehouses and in all to which you set your hand, and He will bless you in the land which the LORD your God is giving you."
Deuteronomy 28:8

Dear Lord, I desire Your blessing on what You have given me. Now, I pray, bless the work of my hands. Bless my hands as I minister to the sick; bless my hands as I serve my family. Lord, I claim Your promise in this land in which You have placed me. I know I am not here by chance; it is by Your providence. I will go forth and do Your work, knowing that I have Your blessing.

Help me, Lord, to remember to share the blessings You give me and to return to You a faithful portion according to Your word.

*"Blessed is the man who walks not in the counsel
of the ungodly, nor stands in the path
of sinners, nor sits in the seat of the scornful."
Psalm 1:1*

By myself I cannot make good choices. Lord, may Your Spirit guide me as I choose who to spend time with, who to walk with, and who to sit with. Have Your way in my life, and make my heart Your dwelling place. I desire to walk in Your counsel, to walk in the way everlasting, and to always sit at the feet of Jesus.

Forgive my past for my standing in the way of the ungodly and for my sitting in the seat of the scornful. Create in me a dislike for scornful speech and a desire that I may walk in the path of righteousness.

> *"Blessed are all those who put
> their trust in Him."*
> *Psalm 2:12*

It is so luscious to trust in Jesus and to take Him at His word—yes—just to take comfort in knowing His promise and knowing what He says in His Word.

Lord, I pray, bless me that I may always put my trust in You. I realize that I may not always understand; but may I always believe Your word and trust Your grace.

Help me to trust You in good times and in bad. Lead me into a deeper trusting relationship with You. Open my eyes that I may see You when my way is darkened with sorrow, anxiety, or pain. Speak to me in Your still, quiet voice when my world is filled with the noise of doubt and discontent.

> Open my eyes that I may see You when my way is darkened with sorrow, anxiety, or pain.

> *"Blessed is he whose transgression is forgiven, whose sin is covered."*
> *Psalm 32:1*

That this blessing can be mine depends on my choice.

Lord, I choose to believe You, and I ask that You "search me, O God, and know my heart; try me, and know my anxieties; and see if there is any wicked way in me, and lead me in the way everlasting" (Psalm 139:23, 24).

Show me my weaknesses, and may Your grace lead me to repentance. Then forgive my sin and cover me with the blood of Your dear Son. Let this blessing be mine today as You cleanse me according to Your promise. Purify me, transform me, and regenerate my heart and mind.

> *"Blessed is the man to whom the Lord does not impute iniquity, and in whose spirit there is no deceit."*
> *Psalm 32:2*

Father, I am grateful that Jesus has already paid for my sins and that You have now imputed His righteousness to me. I ask that You guide my heart to the truth so that no deceit may be in my spirit. Sanctify me in Your truth, and put to death anything that will hinder me from living a sanctified life.

Help me now to live a sanctified life, one that gives glory to Your name. Let my words, actions, and motives bring honor to You. Guide my steps, and do not lead me into temptation. Let my life reveal the blessing that I have in You.

"Blessed is the nation whose God is the Lord, the people He has chosen as His inheritance."
Psalm 33:12

I am blessed to know that You have no favorites and that I am included in the nation You have chosen as our inheritance.

You say in Your Word that we are a chosen generation, a royal priesthood, a holy nation, and that we are Your own special people. Now guide my steps that I may proclaim Your praises, for You have called me out of darkness into Your marvelous light. Thank You for showing me mercy. Now help me to be obedient to the word to which I am appointed.

> *"Oh, taste and see that the Lord is good,
> blessed is the man who trusts in Him."*
> *Psalm 34:8*

Lord, I don't know what tomorrow will bring or what You have planned for me when I face future challenges nor do I know where Your Spirit will lead me. I don't know by what means You will provide for my needs in the coming days. But, I do know how You have provided in the past. So, I will have peace in knowing that I have nothing to fear for the future unless I forget Your leading in the past.

I rejoice in knowing that You hold tomorrow and that You hold my hand. Great is Your faithfulness. All I have ever needed—or that I will ever need—Your hand will provide. Surely, my tomorrow will be great! Amen.

> *"Blessed is that man who makes the LORD his trust, and does not respect the proud, nor such as turn aside to lies."*
> *Psalm 40:4*

I will put my trust in You because I know that I have Your promise, "Be anxious for nothing, but in everything by prayer and supplication, with thanksgiving, let your requests be made known to God" (Phil. 4:6). Help me to always make my wants and wishes known to You.

In You, O Lord, I will find relief in times of distress and grief; in You I will find comfort for my troubled soul. In You I will find refuge and escape the tempter's snare. All You ask me to do is to believe Your word and trust Your grace. Upon You, I cast all my cares and I wait lest I turn aside to lies.

*"Blessed is he who considers the poor,
the LORD will deliver him in time of trouble.
The LORD will preserve him and keep him alive,
and he will be blessed on the earth."*
Psalm 41:1

Open my heart that I may feel the need to help the poor. Your people hunger and thirst for love; help me to find a place for them in my heart. Help me to give part of my time to be with the lonely. Help me to speak an encouraging word to the despondent. Help me to have a cheerful countenance and a smile on my face. Sometimes that is all I need to give.

Out of the abundance of Your blessings to me, bless me with a cheerful heart that I may share with those who are in need. I desire to be a blessing to others because I know that Your hand has delivered me from trouble. Keep me alive in the faith, for that is the only way I can consider the poor.

> *"Blessed are those who keep justice,*
> *and he who does righteousness at all times!"*
> *Psalm 106:3*

It has been said: "Conscience is the chamber of justice" (Origin). So I submit to the leading of the Holy Spirit. I ask that I be transformed by the renewal of my mind that I may be empowered to "prove what is that good and acceptable and perfect will of God" (Romans 12:2).

May the One who is the author and finisher of my faith help me to lay aside all that leads to injustice and unrighteousness. Bless me that I may do justly, love mercy, and walk humbly before You.

Holy Spirit, have Your way in my life. Come and take control of my thoughts, my feelings, and my emotions. Quiet my spirit and lead me all the way. Hear my cries and unspoken needs and make them known to the Father.

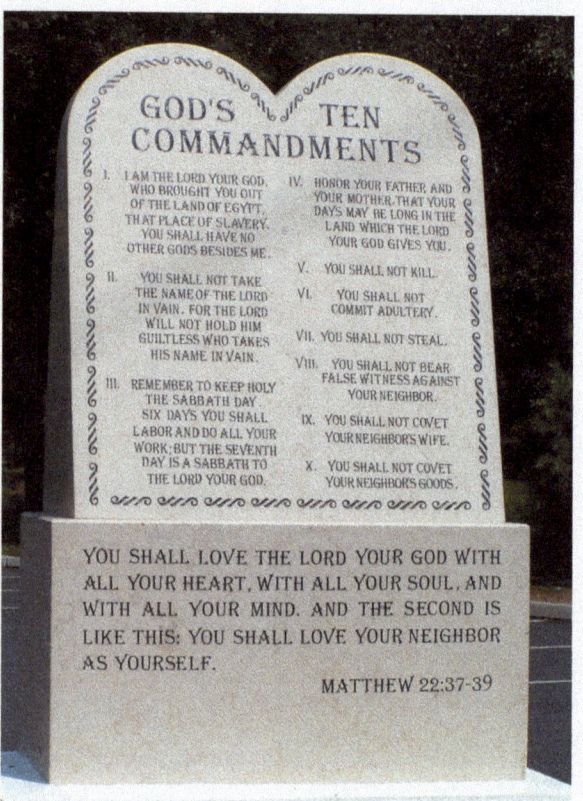

"Blessed is the man who fears the LORD, who delights greatly in His commandments."
Psalm 112:1

O Lord, open my lips, and my mouth will declare Your praise. Let me delight in Your law and help me to meditate upon Your goodness and Your majesty.

Father, I want to exalt You because You are my God. There is no one like You. Lord, You rule, You reign, and there has never been and never will be anyone like You. Daddy, You are awesome, wonderful, and marvelous.

I will praise Your name for all the wonderful things You have done in my life. Your admonitions of old are faithful and true. You are strength to the poor, and you give strength to the needy in distress. You shelter me from the storm and provide a shadow from the heat.

> *"Blessed are the undefiled in the way,*
> *who walk in the law of the LORD."*
> Psalm 119:1

Dear Lord, it is my heart, my desires, my feelings, my attitudes, and my choices that keep me from walking in Your law. Bless me with a new heart and a renewed spirit that I may be undefiled. Help me to understand that the things that are outside of me have no influence upon my character as the things that originate from within me.

As Your Word clearly stipulates, out of the abundance of my mouth I will speak and act. Therefore, Lord, come now and have Your way in my life. Transform me by regenerating my mind. Silence any impure thoughts. Fill me with praises for Your goodness, and sanctify my desires. I will fix my eyes on You, Lord, please perfect my faith.

> *"Blessed are those who keep His testimonies,*
> *who seek Him with the whole heart."*
> *Psalm 119:2*

To do Your will, O my God, is my desire; Your law is within my heart. "I do not hide your righteousness in my heart; I speak of your faithfulness and your saving help. I do not conceal your love and your faithfulness from the great assembly" (Ps. 40:9, 10, NIV).

"And you will seek Me and find Me, when you search for Me with all your heart" (Jer. 29:13). "But from there you will seek the LORD your God, and you will find Him if you seek Him with all your heart and with all your soul" (Deut. 4:29).

Holy Father, please show me the rooms in my heart that I have not given to You. Take my life, and let it be consecrated to thee. Take my feet, my hands, my lips, my voice, my will, and my heart. Take my silver; take my love and take myself, and I will be ever only for thee. Lord, I surrender all.

> *"Blessed is every one who fears the LORD,*
> *who walks in His ways."*
> *Psalm 128:1*

When we walk with the Lord, when we do His good will, what a glory He sheds on our way! There are times I have tried to walk on my own, and I have always failed. I want to walk in Your ways, Lord, but it is not easy.

I lift up my voice to You and pray. O let me walk with thee, my Lord. If I walk alone, I cannot stand the tempests that rage my way or the snares that beset my feet. Take my hand, precious Lord, and linger thou near me.

Help me to uphold Your Word as a lamp unto my feet. Walk with and talk with me all the way. One thing I ask of You, do not let me doubt Your tender mercies, for throughout life You have been my guide.

> *"Now therefore listen to me, my children,
> for blessed are those who keep my ways."*
> *Proverbs 8:32*

Lord, I realize that I don't take time to listen to You. There is so much noise around. There are many voices that compete for my attention. Help me to recognize Your voice when You speak. Help me to slow down and get to know You well. I need to spend time with You; that is the only way I can identify Your voice.

Help me to shun the things in my life that make it difficult for me to hear Your voice. Then bless me with a desire to keep Your ways; Your ways are perfect. Lead me gently lest I fall to the wayside.

> *"Blessed is the man who listens to me,*
> *watching daily at my gates waiting*
> *at the posts of my doors."*
> *Proverbs 8:34*

My heart is inclined to listen to the adversary. I will not naturally choose to listen to Your voice. So, Lord, I pray that You work in me both to will and to do of Your good pleasure. Cause me to listen to Your voice. Bring to completion the good work You have started in me.

Lead me to set my mind on things that are above; let my life be hidden in Christ. Apart from You, I can do nothing. I choose to abide in You. I will watch, wait, and look unto You for guidance.

Help me to set aside time to read Your Word. Speak to me, rebuke me, instruct me, teach me, and reveal Yourself to me through Your Word.

> *"Blessed are the poor in spirit,
> for theirs is the kingdom of heaven."*
> Matthew 5:3

Poor, pitiful, blind, and naked is my true condition. But I realize there are times I behave like I am self-reliant, that I can do without You. Now I ask that, by Your grace, You may open my eyes to the fact that, without You, I am incapable of accomplishing anything.

It is by depending on You every day that I am assured of victory. When Israel depended on past victory and went to war without Your blessing, they were defeated. Help me to learn from their experience and keep my focus on You. Help me to put to death the members within me that feel not the need to be led by You.

> *"Blessed are those who mourn,*
> *for they shall be comforted."*
> Matthew 5:4

Lead me to have a deep sorrow for my sins. Let me not be comfortable in sin. There is so much evil going on, and my heart is inclined to see that it is normal for things to be the way they are.

You have loved me with unspeakable tenderness, yet my life has been filled with ingratitude and rebellion. Forgive me and draw me unto Yourself. May the trials of my life work to cleanse the impurities of my life and smooth the roughness of my character.

Though the road be rough, I will keep on going. For, "the LORD is my shepherd; ... though I walk through the valley of the shadow of death, I will fear no evil; for You are with me; Your rod and Your staff, they comfort me" (Psalm 23:1, 4).

> *"Blessed are the meek, for they
> shall inherit the earth."*
> *Matthew 5:5*

Bless me with the mind of Christ. Kill the desire for revenge in me. Create in me a forgiving heart and make me patient and gentle to those who wrong me.

My human condition struggles for attention and expression; it is always ready for contest. Lord, help me to learn to empty myself of pride and all desire for supremacy so I can have silence in my soul. Make my heart yield to the disposal of Your Holy Spirit.

Anytime I feel anxious and desire the highest place, remind me to not let my ambition crowd and elbow myself into notice but let me remember that my highest place is at the feet of Jesus my Savior. Make me look to Jesus and wait for His hand to lead me and to listen for His voice to guide me.

"Blessed are those who hunger and thirst for righteousness, for they shall be filled."
Matthew 5:6

My body needs water and food to survive.

As I need food to sustain my physical strength, so do I need Christ, the Bread of life who came from heaven, to sustain my spiritual life and to impart strength that I may perform the works of God.

I eat every day—two or three times, in fact. As my body is frequently receiving the pabulum that sustains life and vigor, so my soul must be regularly communing with Christ, submitting to Him and depending wholly upon Him. As the weary sojourner seeks for a spring in the desert to quench his burning thirst, so do I need thirst for the pure water of life, of which Christ is the fountain.

Breathe on me, Lord; make my desire be for You. Feed me till I want no more. "Open now thy crystal fountain, whence the healing stream doth flow." Bless me with a longing after Your heart.

> As I need food to sustain my physical strength, so do I need Christ, the Bread of life who came from heaven, to sustain my spiritual life and to impart strength that I may perform the works of God.

> *"Blessed are the merciful, for they
> shall obtain mercy."*
> *Matthew 5:7*

I need surgery. By nature, my heart is cold and dark and unloving; whenever I do anything, the intent is for me to be seen and praised. Now, Father, take this cold heart of mine and replace it with a kind, loving, and forgiving heart that only You can give.

There are many to whom life is a painful struggle, who feel that they are deficient, are miserable and unbelieving. Lord, help me to be a blessing to such souls. Many in this life feel they have nothing to be grateful for.

Give me kind words, looks of sympathy, and expressions of appreciation. To many struggling and lonely people, these would be as a cup of cold water to a thirsty soul and would lift burdens that rest heavily upon their weary shoulders. Let every word or deed of unselfish kindness be an expression of the love of Christ for lost humanity.

> *"Blessed are the pure in heart,*
> *for they shall see God."*
> *Matthew 5:8*

Lord, purify and refine my thoughts and manners. Create in me a growing distaste for careless manners, unseemly language, and coarse thoughts. Purify my heart and my life through the indwelling of the Holy Spirit. Touch my heart, my soul, and my body so that I may live to bring glory to Your name.

Lord, place Your hands on me; breathe thy Spirit on me so I can have the attitude of Jesus in me. Let Your power flow in my heart, and let me reveal the loveliness of Your character in my day-to-day life. Fulfill Your purpose in me and reflect Your image in me as I live among others. Lord, may I never cause a soul to stumble through my words or actions.

May I live as in Your physical presence during the time that You apportion me in the world. Help me to do the right things even when no one is watching me.

*"Blessed are the peacemakers,
for they shall be called sons of God."*
Matthew 5:9

Lord, I repent of the times that I have exhibited hatred and harbored evil surmising in my heart. I pray that the spirit of peace may dwell in me and bring within me a fragrance of life and of loveliness of character, revealing to those around me that I am Your child. Forgive me if I have caused any to stumble in their faith, and revive them according to Your word.

This promise declares a blessing on peacemakers. Lord, I want to be at peace with You and with my fellow men. This is the only way to avoid misery in this life. Let no evil surmising and no hatred prevail in my heart. Cause me to be a partaker of Your heavenly peace and diffuse it to all around me.

> *"Blessed are those who are persecuted for righteousness' sake, for theirs is the kingdom of heaven."*
> *Matthew 5:10*

Father, I am grateful for Your goodness. Thank You for sending your Son to take the blame and for providing a way for us to be acquitted of guilt. I am even more grateful for the sacrifice of Jesus on the cross. He suffered and bled and died so I can be counted righteous.

Now, I ask, give me the strength to endure any kind of suffering for Your cause. Like our forerunners whom Satan tortured and put to death, help me to stand up for You. Cause me to have steadfast faith. Though the body may be tortured and killed, no one can touch a life hid in You. The sufferings of this world are temporary. In difficult times, help me to look beyond the gloom to the glory of the life You have prepared for me.

Lord, while this is true, help me not to be the cause of persecution for other people. Help me not to be the cause of persecution even for myself, only let me live my life in harmony with Your will.

> In difficult times, help me to look beyond the gloom to the glory of the life You have prepared for me.

> *"Blessed are you when they revile
> and persecute you, and say all kinds
> of evil against you falsely for My sake."*
> *Matthew 5:11*

Grant that I may not waste time trying to argue, prove, or explain misunderstandings that have no basis. I ask for grace and wisdom to live—even when there are false rumors going on about me. Keep me away from slanderers and help me not to blacken other people's reputations by spreading false rumors.

Lord, help me to know that, though defamation may blacken my reputation, it cannot stain my character because You are keeping it for me. So long as I do not consent to sin, there is no power, whether human or satanic, that can bring a stain upon my soul. Hence, let me take time to develop character.

Whenever my words, motives, or actions are misrepresented and falsified, let me not mind it, for greater interests are at stake. Give me peace to go through it. Only let me not forsake You.

> *"And blessed is he who is
> not offended because of Me."*
> **Matthew 11:6**

Your answer to John while he was in prison encourages me. You were telling John not to be discouraged even though he was disappointed. I believe this counsel is for me too.

There are times I have been disappointed, discouraged, upset, or angry when my prayers were not answered the way I thought they should have been. Your word is for me not to be discouraged but to hold onto my faith.

The signs of the times denote that the end of all things is at hand. Help me to watch and hold myself in readiness for the coming of the Master at any time. Help me to wait with hope and trust, not neglecting to avail myself of Your instructions, encouragement, and comfort so Your light may shine forth through me into the darkness of the world.

> *"Blessed is she who believed, for there will be a fulfillment of those things which were told her from the Lord."*
> *Luke 1:45*

Mary believed Your word and submitted to Your will. Through her we were blessed with a savior.

In this world saturated by science, I am often tempted to seek to prove that which You have bid me to do. Ours is a generation that walks by sight, but is that which guides us visible?

Now my supplication to You is that You help me to trust and believe Your word even when it doesn't humanly make sense. Bless me with an outlook that affirms, If the Lord says it, it is true. I must learn to walk by faith and not by sight.

"And you will be blessed, because they cannot repay you; for you shall be repaid at the resurrection of the just."
Luke 14:14

The human tendency is to reciprocate in kind. We are good to those who are good to us; we give to those who give to us; we are kind to those who are kind to us, and we love those who love us. But, this is not the principle of Your action.

You loved us when we were Your enemies; You died our death so that we can live Your life. You became poor, so that we can become rich toward God, and by Your wounds we are healed.

Now, I would be like Jesus, in my heart, I want to be more loving, more patient, more hospitable and more forgiving—this time, specifically—to those who may not reciprocate in kind. Give me a heart for humanity, I pray.

> *"If you know these things,
> blessed are you if you do them."*
> John 13:17

The rich young ruler represents many of us. He knew the commandments by heart, but he was not living as he should. He was a good man in society, but his heart was distant from God; he loved his possessions more than he loved those around him.

Knowledge of the truth will not save me. It is in knowing Him who is the Truth and living as He lived that I may have the assurance of living a blessed life.

Give me power, my dear Lord, that I may do all that which I know. Pardon me for wasted moments, unimproved opportunities, and any neglect on my part that has caused a soul not to learn of Your goodness. Let me be a hearer and doer of Your Word. I need to walk in the light revealed to me and not in darkness.

*"Blessed are those who have not seen
and yet have believed."*
John 20:29

Thank You for blessing me ahead of time. You knew I would need this encouragement. Evolution and the Big Bang are some of the human theories that confuse the minds of many.

I believe that You are the Creator of the world, that You came to earth as a babe born of Mary, that You lived amongst us and sinned not, that You died on the cross and rose again for me, that You are now at the right hand of God, and that soon You are coming to take me home to be with You in paradise.

I have not seen You physically, and I cannot prove Your existence scientifically. Yet, one look at my body tells it all—no human could design such an amazing complex. I love You. Keep me in the faith until the day I see You face to face.

"I have shown you in every way, by laboring like this, that you must support the weak. And remember the words of the Lord Jesus, that He said, 'it is more blessed to give than to receive.'"
Acts 20:35

Father, You know how hard it is for me to give my heart to You. It is unnatural. Therefore, I give You permission to come into my heart and do what only You can do. Take my stony heart and give me Your heart of flesh. Create in me a clean heart and a renewed spirit; then I can learn to worship You. Take also my will, my attitudes, and my longings and make them Your own. Only then will I be able to see and support the weak.

Help me to recognize that all I am and all I have is from You. Then cause me to offer sacrifices of thanksgiving to You and give to the poor and needy around me. Help me to give myself, my time, my resources and my talents—just like the good Samaritan—to all humanity irrespective of their race, gender, nationality, or faith.

"Blessed is the man who endures temptation; for when he has been approved, he will receive the crown of life which the Lord has promised to those who love Him."
James 1:12

Father, I am grateful for the strength to overcome temptation as promised in Your Word. Yes, I believe Your Word, which says that no temptation shall befall me except as You shall permit it and that, with every temptation, You have promised a way of escape. Now my prayer is that You will help me to always look to You and not trust my own strength.

I am even more grateful for Your compassion—that You are ever ready to forgive me where I have fallen.

Thanks, Father, for Your grace, Your love and mercy. Lead me to repentance and keep me faithful by Your Holy Spirit till the day of Christ's appearing.

> *"But he who looks into the perfect law of liberty and continues in it, and is not a forgetful hearer but a doer of the work, this one will be blessed in what he does."*
> *James 1:25*

Lord, guard me from vain formality. Help me to accept the power of living faith. Bless me with a willingness to obey all that You want me to do. Open my ears to hear Your call and Your admonition. Give me the strength and courage to do what You want me to do.

I know that sometimes some of Your biddings require me to make changes in my lifestyle. Please help me not to resist Your ways. Cause me to walk in Your path. Though the road may be rough, help me to feel Your presence as I walk the path. I have Your promise.

During those times that people resist my choice for the better, help me to choose You and obey You rather than obeying men. I will fix my eyes on You.

"Blessed is he who reads and those who hear the words of this prophecy, and keep those things which are written in it, for the time is near."
Revelation 1:3

Father, guide me into the truths of the Bible. "This book contains—the mind of God, the state of man, the way of salvation, the doom of sinners, the happiness of believers. Its doctrines are holy; its precepts are binding, its histories are true, and its decisions are immutable." I will "read it to be wise, believe it to be saved, and practice it to be holy" (*Word and Way*, in *Perquiman's Record*, Jan. 14, 1891).

I know that it contains light to direct me and a lamp for my feet. It is food to support me, to comfort, and to cheer me. The Bible is my map and my charter. In it I see paradise restored, heaven opened, and the gates of hell closed. Christ is the eminent subject, my good is its design, and the glory of God is its end.

I will read it slowly, frequently, and prayerfully. It shall be my field of wealth, a bliss of God's glory, and a stream of gratification.

> *"'Blessed are the dead who die in the Lord from now on.' ... 'that they may rest from their labors, and their works follow them.'"*
> *Revelation 14:13*

What better blessing can one have than to die in the Lord? In Scripture, I read about Stephen's kneeling in prayer as he is being stoned. Then, forgiving his persecutors, he dies as he sees heaven open. I desire this blessing, Lord. I want to take my rest, knowing that I have the assurance of seeing You when You come and that those I leave behind shall be encouraged by the fact that I have rested in You.

> My daily choices determine my destiny.

Meanwhile, I know there are choices I have to make. My daily choices determine my destiny. I ask that You help me in my daily walk to make better choices. Help me to choose well and to choose life. Bless me with living faith, and fill my heart. I love You.

> *"Behold I am coming as a thief. Blessed is he who watches, and keeps his garments, lest he walk naked and they see his shame."*
> *Revelation 16:15*

It was business as usual when the rain started falling during Noah's time. But Noah was ready; He had obeyed Your word. Lot believed You when You said that Sodom and Gomorrah would be destroyed. Sudden destruction hit the people who were going about their business. So will it be when You come—Your coming will be unannounced!

Lord, I pray, please guide me in my Christian walk so that I can be ready always. "Just a closer walk with thee" is all I need. Thank You for clothing me with the righteousness of Jesus. I shall not be ashamed unless I denounce Him. May I then be found ready when You come. Show me the things in my life that may leave me unprepared for Your coming. Sanctify my eyes, my ears, and my mouth. Let me live only for thee.

Dear Lord, keep for me what I now commit to You until Jesus comes, that is, my soul.

> ***"'Blessed are those who are called to the marriage supper of the Lamb!'"***
> ***Revelation 19:9***

Everyone is called. I am called to the marriage supper, whether I partake of it depends on me. What is my choice? You call me when You say, "'Come now, let us reason together, ... though your sins are like scarlet, they shall be as white as snow'" (Isaiah 1:18). You call me when You say, "Come to Me, all you who labor and are heavy laden, ... and you will find rest for your souls." Perhaps the highest calling is that You loved the world so much that You gave Your only Son, that, if I believe, I shall not perish but will have everlasting life!

Thank You for providing everything that is needed for the feast that will take place in the first-time venue of the heavenly courts, which no human eye hath ever seen. The food will be served by angels, and the redeemed will eat even of the tree of life. I will be an invited guest, bearing my ticket—the blood of Jesus! I am coming, Lord. Count me in, thanks to my Jesus!

"Blessed and holy is he who has part in the first resurrection. Over such the second death has no power, but they shall be priests of God and of Christ, and shall reign with Him a thousand years."
Revelation 20:6

    Lord, Your Word proclaims that You will descend from heaven surrounded by the glory of myriads of angels. Then, at Your command, the angels will sound the trumpets. The ears of the righteous dead will be opened, and they will hear Your voice. They will emerge from their graves victorious. Then, You will give them new bodies with the ability to fly, and they will greet You in the clouds.

This is my desire, my hope. I have the assurance that Jesus died and rose again for me. Bless me that I may be part of those who are raised from the dead. Help me to never lose sight of this assurance from Your Word. Though this life I may lose, let me experience the resurrection at Your return. Comfort me with these words of promise whenever I lose a loved one. Help me to proclaim this truth to others in Your name.

> Though this life I may lose, let me experience the resurrection at Your return.

> *"'Behold, I am coming quickly!*
> *Blessed is he who keeps the words*
> *of the prophecy of this book.'"*
> Revelation 22:7

Come, Lord Jesus; come into my heart. Come in today; come in to stay. Come and make me new; come and walk with me. Come and rule my life; come and set me free, for then I can joyfully declare: *Come into the world; come and take us home. Come and make the earth new.*

The understanding of the Scriptures, the desire to read them, and the ability to live and do what they say come from You. I now submit to Your will, oh Lord. Bless me with Your Holy Spirit. May Your Word instruct, teach, rebuke, exhort, and train me in the principles of Your kingdom.

Instruct me in Your way; lead me in what is right, for You are good and upright. Bless me by putting away from me every false way; graciously teach me Your law. Then I will teach transgressors Your way.

> *"Blessed are those who do His commandments, that they may enter the right to the tree of life, and may enter through the gates of the city."*
> *Revelation 22:14*

By myself I cannot keep the commandments; I cannot meet the demands of Your law. I rejoice in knowing that that which the law could not do You did for me. This blessing is easy, I will let You live our Your life within me, and I will abide in You. If I try, I will fail terribly and I will not eat of the tree of life.

My supplication to You now is, "come Thou Fount of every blessing"—come and tune my heart to sing Your praises. I am prone to wander; I am prone to leave You. So now, Father, take my heart and "seal it for Thy courts above." On that day, let me see You face to face, as You take me to the tree of life. I shall eat of its fruit, and I will live with You for eternity.

"Now it shall come to pass, if you diligently obey the voice of the LORD your God, to observe carefully all His commandments which I command you today, that the LORD your God will set you high above all nations of the earth."
Deuteronomy 28:1

Father, I have Your word and Your promise. But there is a part I need to play; I must choose to obey You. So now I come to You and ask for wisdom. Give me power to make the right choices, power to conquer self.

Bless me with a heart that is willing to obey. Take the stony heart of mine and give me Your heart of flesh. Only then will I truly obey; only then will fertility, prosperity, success, and security be mine. And I will testify of Your goodness. Let other people see Your goodness through my obedience, and may they be drawn to You that they may also receive blessings and be led to obey You.

> Bless me with a heart that is willing to obey.

> *"The LORD will establish you as a holy people to Himself, just as He has sworn to you, if you keep the commandments of the LORD your God and walk in His ways."*
> *Deuteronomy 28:9*

Thank You for Your promise to establish me. I will do what You want me to do, say what You want me to say, and go where You want me to go. Doing so is only possible in You. Apart from You, I can do nothing. Lord, establish me in the faith; make me holy. Then I will be able to keep Your commandments.

In You alone lie my security, confidence, and trust. Take my spirit of restlessness and resistance, which can never wait. Give me Your spirit of calmness and obedience—the meek Spirit of Christ. He loved not Himself but was obedient unto death. I believe that You love me, and I know that, in Your everlasting arms, I will find strength and peace.

"Then all peoples of the earth shall see that you are called by the name of the LORD, and they shall be afraid of you. And the LORD will grant you plenty of goods, in the fruit of your body, in the increase of your livestock, and in the produce of your ground, in the land of which the LORD swore to your fathers to give you. The LORD will open to you His good treasure, the heavens, to give the rain to your land in its season, and to bless all the work of your hand. You shall lend to many nations, but you shall not borrow. And the LORD will make you the head and not the tail; you shall be above only, and not be beneath, if you heed the commandments of the LORD your God, which I command you today, and are careful to observe them. So you shall not turn aside from any of the words which I command you this day, to the right or the left, to go after other gods to serve them."
Deuteronomy 28:10–14

In reading these verses, I notice the following outcome of blessing: All the people of the earth will see that I am called by Your name. So, sustain me, Lord, in the faith lest I stumble and make others fall.

I also notice that You will grant me plenty of goods. Cause me to share with those in need from the abundance that You shall give me. You promise to open Your good treasure from the heavens to give me rain in its season. You will make me the head and not the tail and bless me with success. Cause me, O God, to know that true success is in learning to be like Jesus.

Dear Lord, I realize that I have been a hindrance to my blessings because of some of the choices I have made. Now forgive me, I pray. Let me rejoice in the abundant blessings that You have given me.

> *"Jabez cried out to the God of Israel,*
> *'Oh, that You would bless me indeed,*
> *and enlarge my territory!'"*
> *1 Chronicles 4:10*

God of Israel, enlarge my territory, coast, and borders. Increase my understanding and knowledge of Your Word. Increase my control over evil desires and over my domain. Increase the sphere of my influence to those You bring into contact with me. As You enlarged the coast of Jabez, as You gave David victory over Goliath, give me victory over the things that appear to be giants in my life.

Thank You for the talents You have given me. Grant me opportunities to use them to the glory of Your name. Use my limitations to prosper Your Kingdom. Open my heart to those in darkness. Reveal to me all the avenues and opportunities for witnessing, and give me the courage to tell others of Your goodness. Make me a blessing, a humble instrument in Your service.

> *"Jabez cried out to the God of Israel,
> 'Oh, ... that Your hand would be with me.'"*
> 1 Chronicles 4:10

Your hand, oh God, is a sign of power, strength, and victory. It is a sign of divine guidance, yes, of Your divine presence. Your hand is mighty to create, save, heal, and protect. Your hand provides for my needs. Your hand guides into safety and helps those who are lost to find their way.

Therefore, I pray, let Your hand be upon me. Here I am, Lord. Guide me, teach me, lead me, and heal me. Be involved in the affairs of my life. I need You every hour. Without You, I will stumble and fall. Encourage me and protect me by Your hand.

By Your hand recreate and transform me into Your likeness. Work in me, with me, and through me to advance Your kingdom. Help me to abide in You, to trust You with all my heart, and to watch and wait.

*"Jabez cried out to the God of Israel,
'Oh, that You would ... keep me from evil.'"*
1 Chronicles 4:10

Father, keep me from the things that will lead to my destruction. You understand my frailties and how poorly I make choices. Protect me by helping me to have a solid foundation in Christ.

Help me to be close to You, and create in me a hatred for evil. Put Your hedge around me, and let me feel Your presence. Guide me that I may love the things You love and hate the things You hate.

Help me also to fix my eyes on You when I am down in the valley. Help me not to doubt Your goodness. Help me to know that the circumstances that surround me are not an announcement of Your intentions towards me.

I have confidence in Your faithfulness. I believe that You will establish me and guard me from the evil one and that You will direct my heart into Your love and into the patience of Christ.

> *"Jabez cried out to the God of Israel,
> 'Oh that You would bless me indeed ...
> that I may not cause pain!'"*
> 1 Chronicles 4:10

Lord, I am thankful that You care about me when I am in pain. I will bring You all my cares. As I pray that You keep me from pain, guide me so that I may not cause pain to anyone else. Bless me with a heart sensitive to other people's feelings. Let me do and be for others what I would want them to do or be for me. Let me not cause pain through my words or my actions.

Lord, enable me to speak in such a way that every word of mine may make a sad heart lighter. Empower me to care, to love, and to be kind. Suffer me to be a friend to the lonely and to bring hope to the despondent. Do for Your people whatever You will through me.

> *"Jabez cried out to the God of Israel,*
> *'Oh that you would bless me indeed ...'*
> *So God granted him what he requested."*
> 1 Chronicles 4:10

Whatever challenges I am facing now, whatever pain I may experience, I will tell it to Jesus. If ever I am weary and heavy laden, I will tell it to Jesus. He is a friend so close, a friend so dear. All my trials and temptations I will take to the Lord in prayer. Jesus can and will answer me. He heard the cry of Jabez; He will hear my cry too.

I lift Your name on high because You have answered so many prayers. Good Lord, Your blessings are abundant, and You have done so much for me. I can tell of Your mercy, Your love, Your protection, and Your guidance. I can tell of Your safety and testify of Your healing power. I can tell how You have comforted me and given me peace in moments of distress. Yes, I can tell how You have encouraged me and given me hope.

Oh, magnify the name of the Lord. To the Lord God be the glory!

And now, Lord, I pray, please bless me with:

- A loving heart that I may accommodate those who make it difficult for me to love them
- A forgiving spirit that I may forgive those who wrong me, not keeping a record of evil
- A kind heart that I may show mercy to those in need

- A willing heart that I may do what You want me to do, say what You want me to say, and go where You want me to go
- A cheerful countenance that I may bring hope to the discouraged
- A grateful spirit that I may sing praises to Your holy name
- A discerning mind that I may tell right from wrong, approve the things that are excellent, and act sincerely and without offense till the day of Christ
- Wisdom that I may know how to guide the children that You have placed under my care
- Patience that I may be able to stand in faith even in difficult times
- The mind of Christ that I may be humble and teachable
- An attitude of gratitude that I may not complain or grumble
- The desire to seek peace and pursue it, displacing the desire for revenge
- A mind set on things above that I may not crave the earthly things that perish
- The gift of generosity that I may give out of the abundance of Your blessings
- Contentment in all things and conduct without covetousness
- The fruits of righteousness, which are by Jesus Christ, to the glory and praise of God
- Affection for my spouse and freedom from any desire for any other that I may keep our marriage bed undefiled
- The peace of God which defies all human reasoning.
- No fellowship with the unfruitful works of darkness except to expose them
- The blessing of conduct worthy of the gospel of Christ
- A pure and undefiled heart, out of the abundance of which the mouth speaks

- Patience so that I can be tolerant of the mistakes of others, knowing that You are working in them as much as You are in me
- Self-control to enable me to overcome all evil propensities
- My family's daily needs, for You are our shepherd and provider, and in You we lack for no good thing
- A desire to be in Your presence now and throughout eternity, thanking You for the home that You have prepared, yet living in your presence throughout this life. Amen.

We invite you to view the complete
selection of titles we publish at:
www.TEACHServices.com

We encourage you to write us
with your thoughts about this,
or any other book we publish at:
info@TEACHServices.com

TEACH Services' titles may be purchased in
bulk quantities for educational, fund-raising,
business, or promotional use.
bulksales@TEACHServices.com

Finally, if you are interested in seeing
your own book in print, please contact us at:
publishing@TEACHServices.com

We are happy to review your manuscript at no charge.

www.ingramcontent.com/pod-product-compliance
Lightning Source LLC
Chambersburg PA
CBHW042134160426
43199CB00021B/2908